YOU HAVE THE POWER TO BE GREAT!

A Christian Empowerment Workbook

DR. NORA SHARIFF-BORDEN

"For greater is He that is in me than he that is in the world."
1 John 4:4 NIV

Updated Edition

For greater is He that is in me than he that is in the world. What a powerful reminder that I never walk alone. The One who lives inside of me is greater than any challenge, obstacle, fear, or opposition that I may face. He protects me, guides me, loves me, and gave His life for me so that I could live in freedom and victory.

Because He resides within me, I am reminded of my worth, my purpose, and the greatness He has placed inside of me. He continually shows me that I have been created with the ability to accomplish what He has called me to do. Through Him, I have the power to rise above limitations, overcome difficulties, and walk confidently in my God given purpose.

My faith is not in my own strength, wisdom, or ability. My faith is in Him and Him alone. The greater One lives within me, and because of that, I can move forward with courage, confidence, and unwavering trust, knowing that He will lead me every step of the way.

"Greater is He that is in you than he that is in the world."
1 John 4:4 NIV

Special Thanks

A special thank you to my Lord and Savior, who believed in me when I did not yet believe in myself. When I doubted my value, You reminded me that I was chosen. When I questioned my purpose, You whispered destiny into my spirit. When I thought I had nothing to offer, You breathed greatness into me. You placed words within my heart and gently said, "Write." Because of You, I discovered gifts I never knew were there. Because of Your grace, I found courage to move forward. Because of Your love, I learned that with You all things are possible. Lord, I love You with all my heart, and I thank You for every open door, every lesson, every blessing, and every moment You show me that I have the power to be great.

To my mother, thank you for showing me what strength looks like. You taught me greatness by the way you lived your life. You faced challenges that could have broken many, yet you kept rising. You stood tall when life became difficult. You kept moving when others would have given up. Your perseverance became a blueprint for my own life. You taught me that circumstances do not define me, that my faith, determination, and courage do. Thank you, Mom, for being an example of resilience, dignity, and excellence.

To my best friend and husband, Neil, thank you for your steadfast support and unconditional love. Thank you for allowing me to be fully myself with no conditions attached. Thank you for standing beside me through seasons of joy, challenge, growth, and victory. Forty-seven years of love and friendship has been a blessing I will never take for granted. You are a wonderful husband, a devoted father, grandfather, and a wise teacher. Your loyalty and love have been a gift in my life. I thank God for the bond we share, and I love you deeply.

To my pastor, Rev. Dr. Cynthia Hale, you are truly my spiritual mentor. You have not only preached the Gospel of Jesus Christ, but you have lived it before the people. Your walk has spoken as loudly as your words. Your obedience, wisdom, compassion, and commitment to God have left a deep and lasting impact on my life. I am grateful for every sermon, every prayer, every word of encouragement, and every example of faithfulness. Thank you for continuing to allow God to use you to bless my life and the lives of so many others. May God continue to strengthen and favor you.

To my children, I love you with the love of Christ. You are each a blessing and a part of my legacy. My prayers are always with you, and my desire is to see each of you walk in purpose, favor, strength, and joy. Never forget that you are loved beyond measure.

To my grandchildren, you are a gift from God, and I am committed to showing you what greatness looks like.

To my sisters, thank you for being my sisters not only by blood, but also by faith. We are truly sisters in Christ, and that bond is precious. Thank you for the laughter, support, prayers, memories, and love we have shared through the years. I am grateful for each of you, and I pray God's continued blessings over your lives.

To Dominé Phillips, thank you for all your talents and support in helping me pull together the final touches of this workbook. God bless you.

To Beth Branning, thank you for your love, counseling, teaching, and for allowing the Holy Spirit to use you to change my life and the lives of all His people. May God continue to bless you with your new ministry, Safe Harbor Ministries. I love you and God bless you.

To God be all the glory for every chapter written and every blessing still to come.

From the Heart of Dr. Nora Shariff-Borden

Dear Sister,

I believe with all my heart that when God blesses us, He never intends for the blessing to stop with us. He blesses our lives so that we may become a light, a help, and an encouragement to others. God has placed gifts, wisdom, strength, compassion, and purpose inside each one of us. These treasures were never meant to remain hidden. It is both our privilege and our responsibility to pour into the lives of others what He has so graciously poured into us.

I have made a passionate and intentional decision to become the woman of God that He has called me to be, one day at a time. I understand that greatness is built daily through choices, discipline, faith, and obedience. Every morning that I rise is a new opportunity to begin again, to think higher, to believe stronger, and to use the most powerful gift God has given me, my mind. A renewed mind can change a life, redirect a future, and unlock doors no one thought possible.

I am truly excited and deeply honored to share with you the best of what God has placed within me. I do not take lightly the opportunity to encourage others on their journey. My prayer is that these words strengthen your spirit, renew your confidence, and remind you that you are chosen for more. I believe you will be blessed, and I believe you will walk into the long-term success, peace, joy, and fulfillment that God has for your life.

Winners are not simply those who never fall.
Winners are those who rise again after life has knocked the wind out of them.
They gather their faith, lift their heads, start the race again, and finish strong.

Most people don't want to go through anything and that is why they don't receive anything!

Stand tall in who God created you to be. Walk boldly in your purpose. Trust His timing. Believe in the greatness He placed inside of you.

Blessings,

Dr. Nora Shariff-Borden

Two Fundamentals of a Christian Life

Before we explore the ten steps to greatness, we must lay the foundation. There are two non-negotiables for every Christian who desires to walk in the fullness of what God has for them:

1. **PRAYER IS A MUST.** Prayer is our direct connection to God. He wants to know we are excited about communicating with Him, to be passionate about who He is in our life. Learning to pray is not a burden, it is a privilege.

2. **COMMIT TO READING GOD'S WORD EVERY DAY.** His Word keeps the line of communication open. It is in His Word that He reveals His purpose, His promises, and His power for our lives.

These two practices are the soil in which every other step in this workbook takes root. Do not skip them.

STEP ONE

Turn Yourself On! Get EXCITED! STAY Excited!

Give yourself permission to be excited about your faith. Many of us have been taught that being enthusiastic about God is somehow inappropriate. But the truth is: God gets excited about our praise! That should tell us everything about how God feels about us praising Him.

> *"Praise the Lord. Praise the Lord, you, His servants; praise the name of the Lord."*
> **Psalm 113:1 NIV**

Decide today to give God the highest praise you can offer. Your passion for the Lord is the spark that ignites your excitement, and your excitement is the fuel to your greatness.

What stops you from praising the Lord freely?

____

Are you afraid of what others will think? If so, why?

____

What are some specific ways you can get excited about what God is doing in your life right now?

____

Notes

STEP TWO

Prayer

There is a certain way we should come before God in prayer, not out of ritual, but out of deep reverence and love. You never want God to feel that you take Him for granted. Here are four powerful elements of prayer that will transform your relationship with Him:

ADORATION: Begin by acknowledging who He is. He is the Lord of lords, awesome and mighty, gracious and wonderful. He is the Great I Am. Affirm His greatness before you bring your requests.

CONFESSION: Confess your sins and seek His forgiveness daily. Part of my own daily prayer is simply: 'Lord, forgive me for anything I have done that is displeasing to You.'

THANKSGIVING: Come to Him with a heart overflowing with gratitude. Thank Him for His grace, His mercy, and His faithfulness. Thanksgiving shows God that you appreciate Him, not just what He does for you, but who He is.

SUPPLICATION: Then, with a thankful and believing heart, bring your requests to Him. He is a rewarder of those who diligently seek Him (Hebrews 11:6). Ask, and believe He will deliver.

"But seek ye first the kingdom of God and His righteousness and all these things shall be added unto you."
Matthew 6:33 NIV

God is always saying: 'Come to Me!' Prayer is not a religious duty, it is a love relationship. Make it the first thing you do each morning and the last thing you do each night.

Is prayer one of your weak points? ❐ Yes ❐ No

____

____

Do you pray every day? ❐ Yes ❐ No

Do you feel confident in your prayer life? ❐ Yes ❐ No

If prayer is a weak point, why do you think that is, and what will you do about it?

____

What is one thing you will commit to doing differently in your prayer life starting today?

____

STEP THREE

Do Your Homework: Know God's Word for Yourself

> *"How can a young man keep his way pure? By living according to Your word. I seek You with all my whole heart; do not let me stray from Your commands. I have hidden Your words in my heart that I might not sin against You."*
> **Psalms 119:9-11 NIV**

God's Word is your lifeline. Everything He desires for you is written in His word, His promises, His instructions, His comfort, His correction, and His power. All we have to do is read it.

Years ago, I was in a group discussion with other Christian women when I made a statement about God not giving us more than we can bear. One of the women corrected me rather harshly and I was so crushed. But the very next day, God spoke to my heart and said: 'Nora, you must know My Word for yourself.' He led me to 1 Corinthians 10:13, and I have never been the same since.

What the enemy meant for my embarrassment, God used for my growth. From that day forward, I became committed to knowing God's Word for myself, not just what my pastors, friends, or commentators say about it. I realized I needed to know it for myself.

"I AM NOT INTIMIDATED ANYMORE ABOUT GOD'S WORD! *For God has not given me the spirit of fear, but of power and of love and of a sound mind.*"
2 Timothy 1:7 NIV

Start with one chapter a day. I recommend beginning with the Gospel of John. I guarantee you will fall in love with it and want to read more. Do not let the enemy convince you that it is too complicated. Just begin and God will bring the understanding.

There Is Power in God's Word. Read It. It Changes Everything.

What is your current fear or hesitation about reading God's Word?

____

What commitment will you make right now to begin or deepen your daily reading?

____

Write down a scripture that has recently spoken to your heart:

____

STEP FOUR

Learn to Create a Unique Presence and Consistently Live It

Our ability to be powerful and great flows directly from the Holy Spirit living within us. When we learn to use the gifts, He has given us, we activate the power that God placed inside of us long before we were born.

A unique presence is not arrogance. It is the quiet, confident authority of someone who knows who they are in Christ. It is walking with your head held high, not because of your own accomplishments, but because you know that the God of the universe lives inside of you. It is making a daily decision to walk in your greatness.

David had a unique presence. That is why God chose him. He was a man after God's own heart, not perfect but fully surrendered.

Stop walking around saying things like: 'Woe is me,' 'I don't know my purpose,' or 'I am so lost.'
THE DEVIL IS A LIAR.
The presence of the Lord is upon you. Now walk in it!

"You do not have because you do not ask." Ask God right now what your greatness looks like. He is waiting to show you.
James 4:2 NIV

List 3 things you can do today to begin carrying yourself differently with more confidence in Christ:

1.____

2.____

3.____

List 3 things you need to do to step fully into God's greatness for your life:

1.____

2.____

3.____

STEP FIVE

Learn How to Reach Out and Become Friends with Others

God never designed you for isolation. He designed you for connection. One of the greatest investments you can make in your journey to greatness is building sincere, life-giving friendships.

The most important part of friendship is learning to reach out, relate, and trust. Do not allow painful past friendships to close your heart to the great relationships God has prepared for you. Friendship is never one-sided, and God desires for you to be surrounded by a powerful circle of influence.

My friend Crisette Ellis says it beautifully: 'Show me your friends, and I will show you your future.' Who you spend your time with matters.

Here are the keys to becoming a great friend and attracting great friends:

- Ask sincere questions and genuinely listen to the answers.
- Take a real interest in the needs and feelings of others.
- Be sensitive to where people are emotionally and spiritually.
- Choose to be in the company of like-minded people. Look for God-fearing people who empower and elevate you.
- Stop looking for 'Me Too Friends' who only validate your struggles. Find friends who push you forward toward your greatness.

God wants us to fellowship. He wants us to grow together, sharpen each other, and celebrate each other's greatness.

Do you tend to pull away from building close friendships? ❐ Yes ❐ No

If yes: What experience has caused that, and are you ready to let God heal you?

___

Describe the kind of friend you want to be and the kind of friends you are asking God to send you:

___

STEP SIX

Discover Who You Are As a Christian

> *"Delight yourself also in the Lord, and He shall give you the desires of your heart."*
> **Psalms 37:4 NIV**

One of the most important journeys you will ever take is the journey inward, discovering who God made you to be. Not who the world says you are. Not who your past says you are. But who God says you are.

As Christians, we are motivated by God's desire for us to achieve and flourish as He has called us to be. To discover what God wants, we must do something beautifully simple: ask Him. The way we do that is through daily relationship, through prayer and through His Word.

True success and peace come when we do things God's way. Once we discover who we are in Christ, we must learn to wait on Him to fulfill what He has promised. This can be challenging but the results, when they arrive, are absolutely worth every moment of the wait.

> *"For I know the plans I have for you, declares the Lord, plans to prosper you and not to harm you, plans to give you hope and a future."*
> **Jeremiah 29:11 NIV**

Who are you? How would you define yourself right now, honestly?

What makes you stand out? What do you believe God has uniquely placed inside of you?

What do you feel your role is as a Christian woman in your family, community, and the world?

What needs to happen for you to feel truly fulfilled in your life with Christ?

STEP SEVEN

As Christians, We Must Have a Great Attitude

Did you know your attitude is one of the most powerful forces in your life? It determines which road you take, the road God has planned for you, or the detour the enemy has laid as a trap.

"Yesterday is a canceled check.
Tomorrow is a promissory note.
Today is the only cash you have. Spend it wisely."

One busy afternoon, I was locked out of my house. My husband had the garage opener. My daughter had left the spare keys in a friend's car. I had to drive to my husband's job to get the garage opener. The moment I began to feel aggravated, I caught myself and started repeating: 'I am not aggravated. I am not aggravated.' Almost immediately, my attitude shifted. I went from frustration to peace in seconds. That is the power God has given us when we trust the Spirit and not the flesh.

"Your attitude should be the same as that of Christ Jesus."
Philippians 2:5 NIV

You have the power to choose your attitude in every situation. Every. Single. Time.

Describe your attitude honestly. What does it look like on a hard day?

____

How do you feel physically, emotionally, and spiritually when your attitude is aligned with Christ?

____

Write down 3 specific things you can do to redirect your attitude when it goes in the wrong direction:

1.____

2.____

3.____

STEP EIGHT

Your Thoughts and Your Words Help Create Your Power

God's Word tells us in Proverbs 18:21 that the tongue has the power of life and death. That is not a figure of speech, that is a spiritual law. What you say about yourself, to yourself, and over yourself shapes the reality you live in.

I once heard the world-renowned author Michelle McKinney Hammond speak on 'Healing at the Pool' from John 5:3-8. The man at the Pool of Bethesda had been ill for 38 years. When Jesus asked, 'Do you want to get well?' the man's response was full of excuses: 'I have no one to help me… someone always gets there before me.' His circle was the blind, the lame, and the paralyzed. He had surrounded himself with others in the same condition.

Jesus did not engage in the excuses. He gave a command: 'Get up. Pick up your mat and walk.' And the man was healed immediately.

How often do we allow our circumstances or our words to keep us lying at the pool? The enemy knows the power of your tongue better than you do. He listens to what you say and uses your own words against you.

"You are snared with the words of your lips."
Proverbs 6:2 NIV

Start your day with power. Bishop Vashti McKenzie offered this affirmation: 'I stand with anticipation that God is going to do great and marvelous things in me, through me, and for me today.' Those are words worth waking up to.

Here is how to begin transforming your words and thoughts:

- Start every morning asking God what His desires are for you today.
- Create a personal list of faith-filled affirmations and speak them daily.
- Find friends who think and speak life and not lack.
- Read something powerful every single day. The Bible is your best starting point.
- Decide that your circumstances will not determine your outcome.
- Journal through the good times and the challenging ones.
- Envision yourself already living the life you have confessed in faith.

"So is my word that goes out from my mouth: It will not return to me empty but will accomplish what I desire and achieve the purpose for which I sent it."
Isaiah 55:11 NIV

What do you say to yourself on a daily basis? Are your inner words mostly positive or negative? Be honest!

____

Have you given yourself permission to be great?

____

Write 5 powerful, faith-filled affirmations you will begin speaking over yourself every morning:

1.____

2.____

3.____

4.____

5.____

STEP NINE

Give All You Have to Christ and Watch Him Unfold the Greatness in Your Life

It is important for us to experience God in every area of our lives, not just on Sunday mornings, not just during the hard times, but in everything. The first step to experiencing Him fully is making the decision to give everything to Him. Fully. Without holding back.

God is pleased when we trust Him completely. Not just with the easy things, but with the big fears, the old wounds, the unanswered questions, and the dreams that feel too large to carry alone. He is not looking for a part-time surrender. He is asking for all of you.

> *"Trust in the Lord with all your heart and lean not on your own understanding. In all your ways acknowledge Him, and He shall direct your paths."*
> **Proverbs 3:5-6 NIV**

The challenge for many of us is that we give it to God, then turn around and pick it back up. We surrender in prayer, then carry the burden again by noon. Yet here is the beautiful truth: every time you lay it down before Him, you are learning the true meaning of trust.

It may feel challenging when you release it, then reach for it again, but growth is happening in the process. Little by little, surrender becomes your natural posture instead of worry becoming your first response.

When trust becomes natural, peace follows. Your heart becomes lighter, your mind becomes clearer, and you will begin to see all that God has for you.

> *"Ask and it will be given to you; seek and you will find; knock and the door will be opened to you."*
> **Matthew 7:7 NIV**

What areas of your life have you been holding back from God? Be honest with yourself here:

____

Do you truly trust God with all things or just some things? What makes full surrender difficult for you?

____

What must you do to deepen your trust in God and build a more surrendered relationship with Him?

____

STEP TEN

Tithing: It Is Our Obligation

"Will a man rob God? Yet you rob me! Bring the whole tithe into the storehouse, that there may be food in my house. Test me in this, says the Lord Almighty, and see if I will not throw open the floodgates of Heaven and pour out so much blessing that you will not have room enough for it."
Malachi 3:10 NIV

As I asked the Lord what I should say about tithing, He reminded me of something simple and profound. When we tithe, we are telling God that we trust Him. We are acknowledging with our actions, not just with our words, that He is in charge of every area of our lives, including our finances.

God does not need our money. He owns everything. But He desires our obedience and our trust. Tithing is an act of faith. It says: 'Lord, I believe You are my source. I believe Your Word. I believe You will take care of me.'

"But remember the Lord your God, for it is He who gives you the ability to produce wealth."
Deuteronomy 8:18 NIV

I once read a story about a woman who had no job and no financial income. What she did have was talent and time, so she chose to tithe in those areas. She gave her service, her gifts, and her willingness to help where she could. God honored her faithfulness and opened the door for employment, which then gave her the ability to tithe financially. Her story reminds us that God does not ask for what we do not have. He asks for a willing heart and obedience with what is already in our hands. When we give what we have, God knows how to multiply it.

When you truly think about it, 10% is not a lot to give back to the One who gave us life, strength, opportunity, and every blessing we enjoy. Tithing is an act of trust, honor, and gratitude toward God, who is the source of all we have. His Word declares that when we are faithful, He will open the floodgates of Heaven and pour out blessings so great there will not be room enough to receive them. This is not just a principle. It is a promise from God. Take Him at His Word, trust His faithfulness, and watch what He will do in your life.

Do you tithe regularly? ☐ Yes ☐ No

If not, what has held you back, and are you ready to step into obedience in this area?

____

If yes, write down specific ways God has blessed you through your faithfulness in tithing:

____

Notes

Always Seeking God's Greatness (A.S.G.G.)

Use this page to craft your own personal A.S.G.G. Write a living blueprint for pursuing the greatness God has placed inside of you.

MY PURPOSE

Why has God placed you on this earth? What is the driving mission of your life?

____

____

MY VALUES

What qualities and principles define who you are as a woman of God?

____

____

MY VISION

Where do you see yourself in 5 years if you fully walk in God's calling for you?

____

____

MY BELIEFS

What do you believe deeply and truly about yourself, and about God's plans for your future?

MY STRATEGIC PLAN

What are the consistent actions and habits that will move you toward your vision?

MY ONE-YEAR GOALS

What specific, measurable goals will you accomplish in the next 12 months?

MY DAILY COMMITMENTS & SHORT-TERM GOALS

What will you do every single day to honor God and grow toward your greatness?

Notes

You Say / God Says

YOU SAY:	GOD SAYS:
"I can't do it."	You can do all things through Me. Philippians 4:13
"It's not worth it."	It will be worth it. All things work together for your good. Romans 8:28
"I'm not smart enough."	I give you wisdom freely and without finding fault. 1 Corinthians 1:30
"I can't figure this out."	I will direct your steps. Trust Me with all your heart. Proverbs 3:5
"I can't Do It"	Come to Me, and I will give you rest. Matthew 11:28-30
"It's not possible."	All things are possible with Me. Luke 18:27
"I'm afraid."	I have not given you a spirit of fear but of power, love, and a sound mind. 2 Timothy 1:7
"I don't have enough faith."	I have given every person a measure of faith. Use it. Romans 12:3
"God doesn't love me like He loves others."	I am no respecter of persons. What I do for one, I will do for you. Romans 2:11

Eight Steps to Becoming a Successful Conscious Woman of God

Change Your Mind and Watch Your Life Change

1 **Surrender**
I admit that I am powerless in my own strength to improve my life. I need help, God's help. I will stop pretending I can do this alone.

2 **I Believe**
I believe there is a power greater than myself. That power is Jesus Christ. I choose to rely on that power today.

3 **I Am Ready to Be Changed**
I recognize that my own self-defeating thinking has contributed to my unhappiness, fear, and failures. I am ready to change my beliefs and attitudes so that God can transform my life from the inside out.

4 **I Decide to Be Changed**
I will make the decision to surrender my will and my life to God. I ask to be changed, deeply and permanently, by the One who has all power to change anything.

5

I Forgive

I forgive myself for every mistake and every shortcoming. I also choose to forgive every person who has ever hurt me. I release them and I release myself into God's healing.

6

I Ask

I make my specific requests known to God, trusting that He hears every word and that He will fulfill every true need according to His perfect will.

7

I Give Thanks

I thank God in advance, before I see the answer, because I know He is already working on my behalf. My power to overcome every obstacle comes from Him alone.

8

I Dedicate My Life

I have decided to enter into a covenant with God. He is my source, my strength, and my supply. I dedicate myself to serving Him and others with maximum commitment. I go forth today with enthusiasm, excitement, and great expectancy, and I am at peace.

Notes

My Personal Testimony

My story begins 63 years ago in the 6th grade. I was sitting in my classroom when the principal came and pulled me out of my class and placed me in a special needs class. I remember exactly how I felt that day, hurt, embarrassed, ashamed, and completely worthless. That was the enemy's plan for me.

But God had a different plan. He had a ram in the bush. His name was Mr. Nash.

The day I arrived in his classroom; I can remember how I felt when Mr. Nash looked at me and spoke these words that changed the trajectory of my life forever: 'You don't belong here. You are smart, and I am going to work with you.' A year later, I passed the standardized school testing and was placed in a regular 8th grade classroom. How awesome is our God! His plans always work!

But even after that victory, I still doubted myself. Those feelings of insecurity followed me into adulthood. I looked for God's love in all the wrong places. Though I had attended church as a child, I didn't truly know the Lord, and that confusion eventually led me to spend 18 years as a practicing Muslim, searching for God in a mosque where I could not find Him. There was always a void. I never felt truly connected.

Then God used my Mary Kay business to plant the seed of Christianity back into my life. He moved me from Boston, Massachusetts to Durham, North Carolina where I knew absolutely no one. There, He placed a young woman named Beth in my path. She invited me to a Women's Fellowship Day at New Mt. Tabernacle Church, where I sat across from the pastor, Pastor Tessie Jones, and her daughter, Tammie. They invited me to Sunday service.

I attended three Sundays in a row. On the fourth Sunday, God spoke to my heart and said: 'It's time. Give your life back to Me.' The void was filled. My life has never been the same.

God took a little girl who was placed in a special needs class and made her great. He gave her a thriving Mary Kay career. He taught her how to count the blessings He poured into her life. Then one day He breathed a Word into her and said, 'Write,' and she became a bestselling author. In March of 2022, she was awarded an Honorary Doctorate in Philosophy and Business from Trinity International University of Ambassadors.

"What He will do for one, He will do for another.
That is His promise. That is His nature."
Dr. Nora Shariff-Borden

What is your story? Write your testimony. This is the version you would tell another person who needs to know that God has not forgotten them:

____

____

Notes

Notes

Notes

Notes

Notes

Notes

Notes

It is Written

You Need Not Be Afraid

"When I am Afraid, I will put my trust in you." Psalm 56:3 (NIV)

Life Is Victorious

"Watch over your heart with all diligence, for from it flow the springs of life."
Proverbs 4:23

Do All To The Glory Of God

"So whether you eat or drink or whatever you do, do it all for the glory of God."
1 Corinthians 10:31 (NIV)

God You Are My Anchor

"We have this hope as an anchor for the soul, firm and secure. It enters the inner sanctuary behind the curtain." Hebrews 6:19 (NIV)

Nothing Will Be Impossible To You

He replied, "Because you have so little faith. Truly I tell you, if you have faith as small as a mustard seed, you can say to this mountain, 'Move from here to there,' and it will move. Nothing will be impossible for you." Matthew 17:20 (NIV)

Think About Such Things

"Finally, brothers and sisters, whatever is true, whatever is noble, whatever is right, whatever is pure, whatever is lovely, whatever is admirable, if anything is excellent or praiseworthy, think about such things." Philippians 4:8 (NIV)

God Is My Armor

"Therefore, put on the full armor of God, so that when the day of evil comes, you may be able to stand your ground, and after you have done everything, to stand."
Ephesians 6:13 (NIV)

You Have The Power To Be Great

"For the Spirit God gave us does not make us timid, but gives us power, love and self-discipline." 2 Timothy 1:7 (NIV)

My Hope Is In God

"And hope does not put us to shame, because God's love has been poured out into our hearts through the Holy Spirit, whom he has given us." Romans 5:5 (NIV)

Open My Eyes God

"Open my eyes that I may see wonderful things in your law." Psalm 119:18 (NIV)

I Am Happy

"Blessed is the people of whom this is true; blessed is the people whose God is the Lord." Psalm 144:15 (NIV)

God Will Restore

"Return to your fortress, you prisoners of hope; even now I announce that I will restore twice as much to you." Zechariah 9:12 (NIV)

My Trust Is In God

"Since my youth, God, you have taught me, and to this day I declare your marvelous deeds." Psalm 71:17 (NIV)

I Serve A God Of Abundance

"The thief comes only to steal and kill and destroy; I have come that they may have life and have it to the full." John 10:10 (NIV)

My Mind Is On You God

"Set your minds on things above, not on earthly things." Colossians 3:2 (NIV)

I Am Confident In Christ

"Being confident of this, that he who began a good work in you will carry it on to completion until the day of Christ Jesus." Philippians 1:6 (NASB)

There Is Nothing Too Hard For My God

"I am the Lord, the God of all mankind. Is anything too hard for me?" Jeremiah 32:27 (NIV)

Wait On The Lord

"Be still before the Lord and wait patiently for him; do not fret when people succeed in their ways, when they carry out their wicked schemes." Psalm 37:7 (NIV)

My Hope Is In The Lord

"Be strong and take heart, all you who hope in the Lord." Psalm 31:24 (NIV)

I Have Great Faith

"Then he touched their eyes and said, 'According to your faith let it be done to you.'" Matthew 9:29 (NIV)

The Lord Is My Protector

"No weapon forged against you will prevail, and you will refute every tongue that accuses you. This is the heritage of the servants of the Lord, and this is their vindication from me,' declares the Lord." Isaiah 54:17 (NIV)

This Is The Lord's Day

"The Lord has done it this very day; let us rejoice today and be glad."
Psalm 118:24 (NIV)

Christ Is My Strength

"I can do all this through him who gives me strength." Philippians 4:13 (NIV)

My Lord Will Answer

"Lord, I wait for you; you will answer, Lord my God." Psalm 38:15 (NIV)

Lord I Trust You

"Trust in the Lord with all your heart and lean not on your own understanding; in all your ways submit to him, and he will make your paths straight."
Proverbs 3:5–6 (NIV)

Your Ways Are Higher Than All The Earth

"As the heavens are higher than the earth, so are my ways higher than your ways and my thoughts than your thoughts." Isaiah 55:9 (NIV)

We Are What We Think

For as he thinketh in his heart, so is he: Eat and drink, saith he to thee; but his heart is not with thee. Proverbs 23:7 (NIV)

My God Is A Good God

"For the Lord is good and his love endures forever; his faithfulness continues through all generations." Psalm 100:5 (NIV)

Remember This:

Expect a Miracle and God Will Do It!
Excellence Is Not Optional!
Walk by Faith and Not by Sight!
Break Out of Your Cocoon and Soar!
Each Day God Wakes You Is a New Opportunity to Live Life to the Fullest!

Dr. Nora Shariff-Borden
nshariff07@gmail.com
bwotmfg.com

www.ingramcontent.com/pod-product-compliance
Lightning Source LLC
Chambersburg PA
CBHW080247130726
48054CB00023B/186
* 9 7 9 8 9 9 2 5 9 1 5 6 9 *